LEARN to READ

a a a a a a

I have _a_ unicorn.

A MAGICAL SIGHT WORDS & PHONICS ACTIVITY WORKBOOK

FOR BEGINNER READERS

Want free goodies?!

———————————

Email us at

modernkidpress@gmail.com

Title the email "Learn to Read!"
and we'll send some goodies
your way!

Questions & Customer Service:
Email us at modernkidpress@gmail.com!

This book belongs to:

a

Trace the word and say it aloud:

a a a a a a a a a

Write the word:

Complete the sentence with the word:

I have ___ unicorn.

Grab a crayon and color the boxes with the word!

a	am	and
at	and	a
a	at	am
am	a	at
a	and	a

I have **a** unicorn. She has **a** golden horn!

a

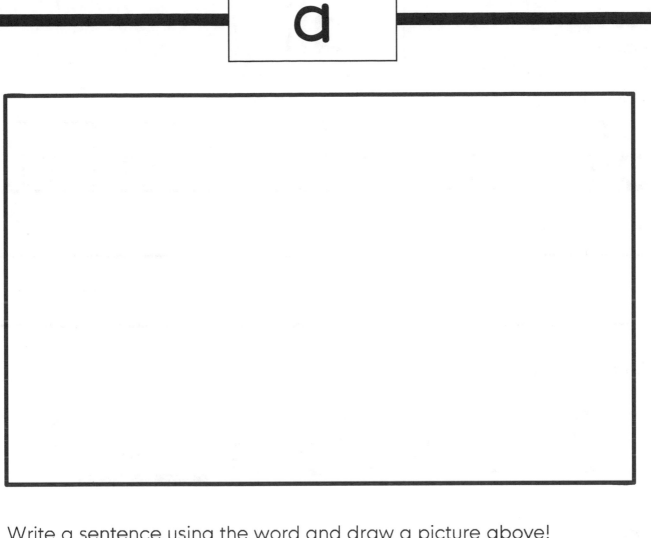

Write a sentence using the word and draw a picture above!

. . . .

. . . .

. . . .

Remember that a sentence begins with a capital letter and ends with a period!

all

Trace the word and say it aloud:

all all all all all all

Write the word:

Complete the sentence with the word:

I can do it ___!

Grab a crayon and color the boxes with the word!

all	am	call
am	all	all
all	ball	am
am	all	call
all	ball	all

I can do it **all**! Be brave
and stand tall!

all

Write a sentence using the word and draw a picture above!

am

Trace the word and say it aloud:

am am am am am

Write the word:

Complete the sentence with the word:

I _____ very sweet.

Grab a crayon and color the boxes with the word!

a	am	and
am	and	am
a	am	and
am	a	at
a	and	am

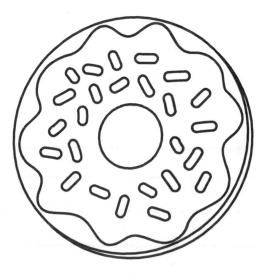

I **am** very sweet. I **am**
a special treat!

am

Write a sentence using the word and draw a picture above!

Remember that a sentence begins with a capital letter and ends with a period!

and

Trace the word and say it aloud:

and and and and

Write the word:

Complete the sentence with the word:

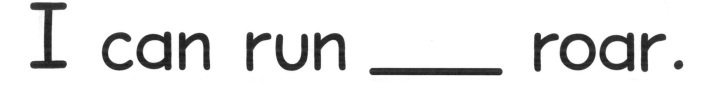

I can run ____ roar.

Grab a crayon and color the boxes with the word!

a	am	and
am	and	am
a	am	and
and	a	at
a	and	am

I can run **and** roar. Now
I am off to explore!

and

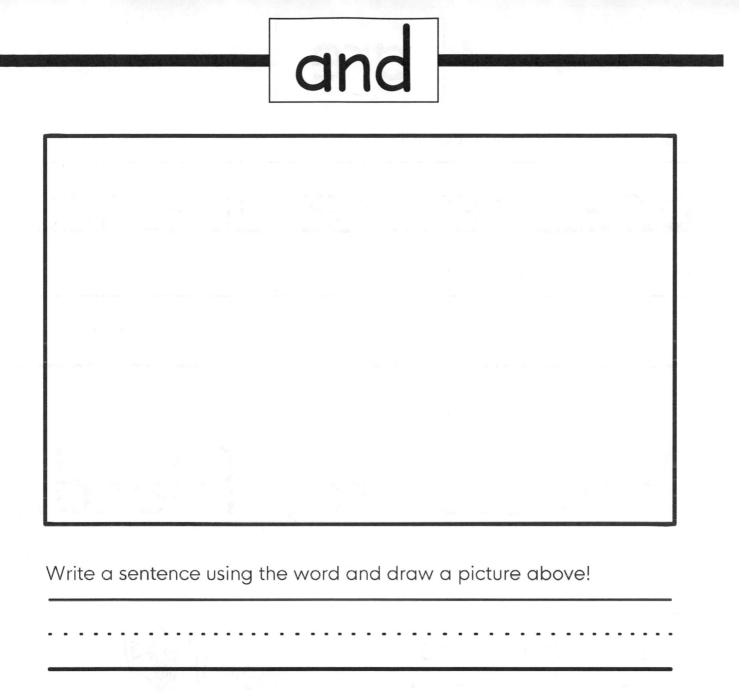

Write a sentence using the word and draw a picture above!

. . . .

. . . .

. . . .

☆ Remember that a sentence begins with a capital letter and
ends with a period! ☆

are

Trace the word and say it aloud:

are are are are are

Write the word:

. . . .

Complete the sentence with the word:

You ____ my friend.

Grab a crayon and color the boxes with the word!

a	am	are
at	are	am
are	am	and
and	are	at
are	a	are

You **are** my friend. I will
love you til the end!

are

Write a sentence using the word and draw a picture above!

Remember that a sentence begins with a capital letter and ends with a period!

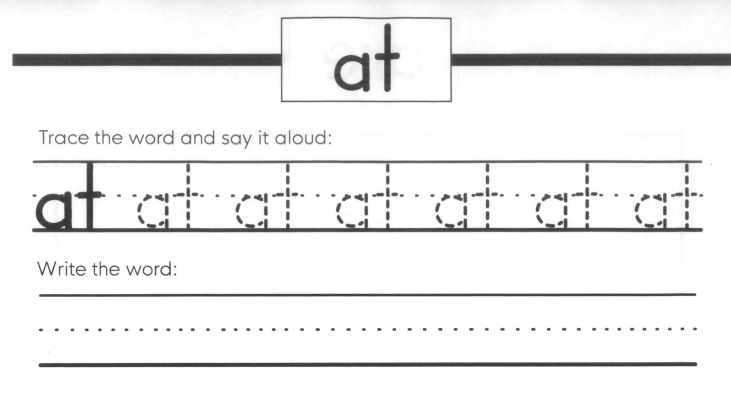

at

Trace the word and say it aloud:

at at at at at at at

Write the word:

Complete the sentence with the word:

I am ___ the castle.

Grab a crayon and color the boxes with the word!

a	at	am
at	are	at
are	at	and
am	are	at
at	a	are

I am **at** the castle. Knock on the door with the tassel!

at

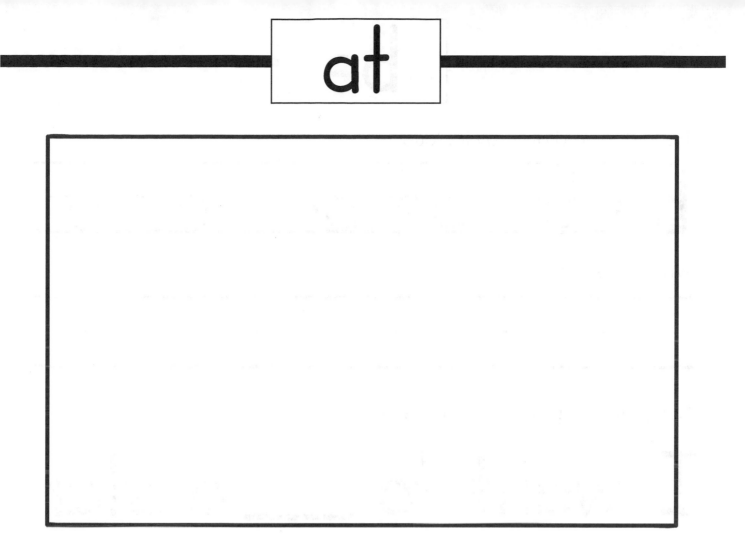

Write a sentence using the word and draw a picture above!

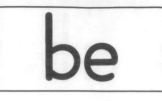

Trace the word and say it aloud:

be be be be be be

Write the word:

Complete the sentence with the word:

I want to ___ a star.

Grab a crayon and color the boxes with the word!

be	big	by
big	be	boy
be	boy	big
by	be	boy
boy	big	be

I want to **be** a star. I will shine near and far!

be

Write a sentence using the word and draw a picture above!

Remember that a sentence begins with a capital letter and ends with a period!

big

Trace the word and say it aloud:

big big big big big

Write the word:

Complete the sentence with the word:

Dinosaurs are ____ .

Grab a crayon and color the boxes with the word!

be	big	by
big	be	boy
be	boy	big
big	be	boy
boy	big	be

Dinosaurs are **big**. Much bigger than a pig!

big

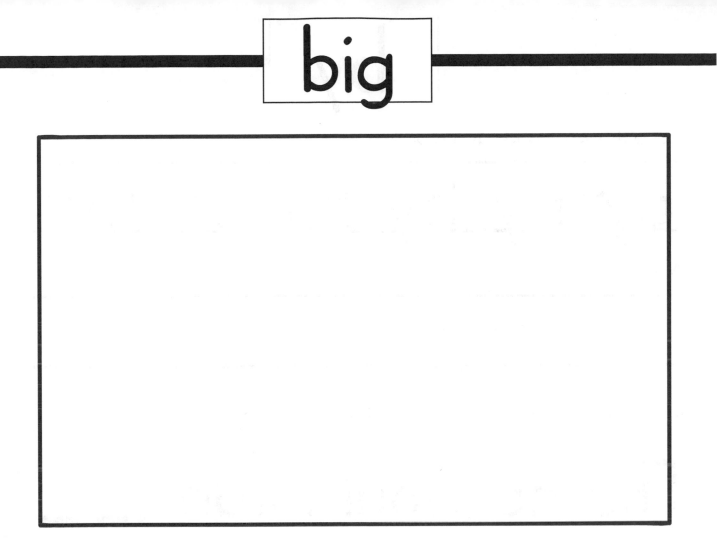

Write a sentence using the word and draw a picture above!

by

Trace the word and say it aloud:

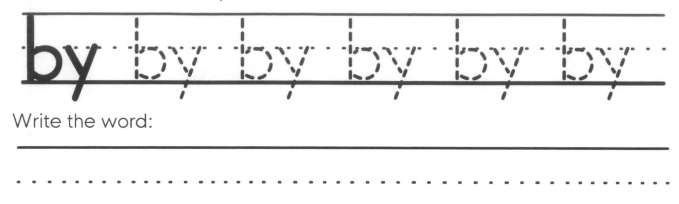

by by by by by by

Write the word:

Complete the sentence with the word:

The narwhal swam ___!

Grab a crayon and color the boxes with the word!

by	be	by
bye	by	be
by	be	bye
bye	by	be
by	bye	be

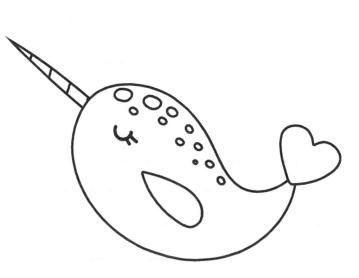

The narwhal swam **by**! She was polite and said, "Hi!"

by

Write a sentence using the word and draw a picture above!

Remember that a sentence begins with a capital letter and ends with a period!

can

Trace the word and say it aloud:

can ˙can˙ ˙can˙ ˙can˙ ˙can

Write the word:

Complete the sentence with the word:

I _____ grow flowers.

Grab a crayon and color the boxes with the word!

can	cat	come
cat	can	car
come	cat	can
car	can	come
can	come	can

I **can** grow flowers. We just
need rain showers!

can

Write a **sentence** using the word and draw a picture above!

⋆ Remember that a sentence begins with a capital letter and ends with a period!

come

Trace the word and say it aloud:

come   come   come

Write the word:

Complete the sentence with the word:

_____ see the rainbow.

Grab a crayon and color the boxes with the word!

can	come	cat
car	can	come
can	come	can
come	car	come
cat	come	can

Come see the rainbow. We can watch the colors glow!

come

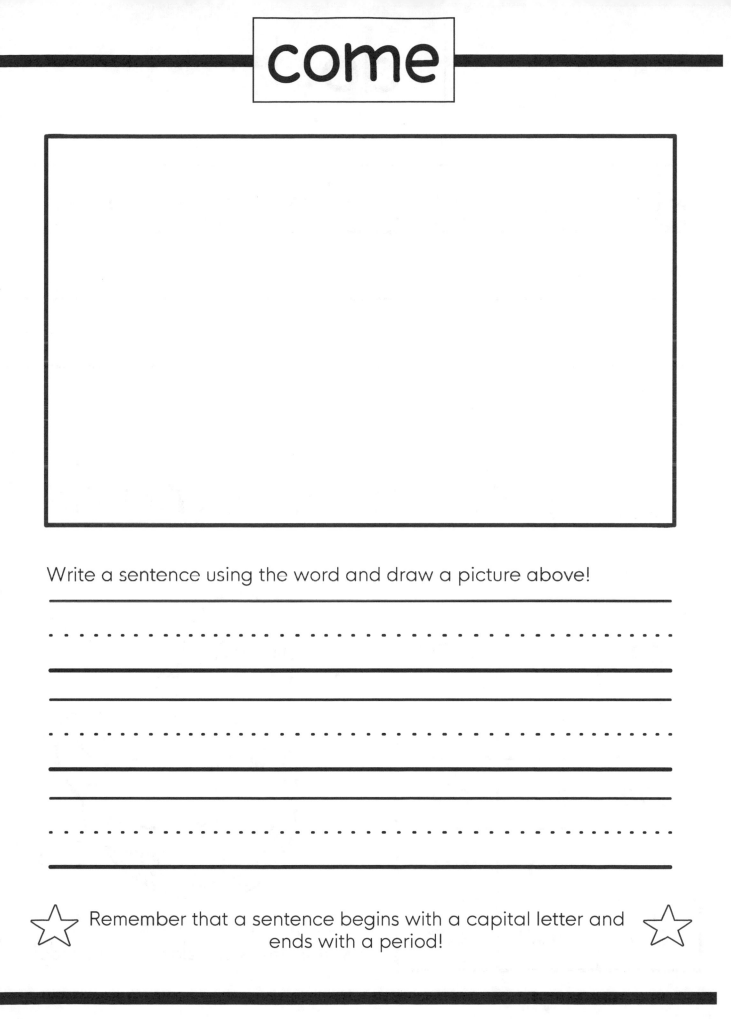

Write a sentence using the word and draw a picture above!

⭐ Remember that a sentence begins with a capital letter and ends with a period! ⭐

Trace the word and say it aloud:

do do do do do do

Write the word:

....

Complete the sentence with the word:

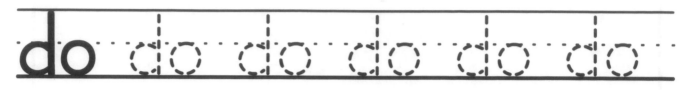

_____ you like mermaids?

Grab a crayon and color the boxes with the word!

do	dot	doe
dot	do	dot
doe	dot	do
dot	do	doe
do	doe	do

Do you like mermaids? Let's swim in the sun, relax in the shade!

do

Write a sentence using the word and draw a picture above!

Remember that a sentence begins with a capital letter and ends with a period!

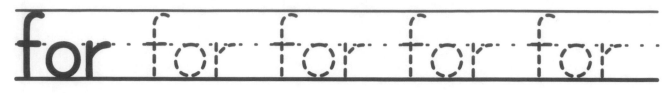

Trace the word and say it aloud:

for for for for for

Write the word:

_____

. . . .

_____

Complete the sentence with the word:

This candy is ____ you.

Grab a crayon and color the boxes with the word!

for	of	off
off	for	four
for	four	for
of	for	off
four	of	for

This candy is **for** you. It will turn your mouth blue!

for

Write a sentence using the word and draw a picture above!

. . . .

. . . .

. . . .

Remember that a sentence begins with a capital letter and ends with a period!

go

Trace the word and say it aloud:

go go go go go go

Write the word:

Complete the sentence with the word:

Let's ___ swimming.

Grab a crayon and color the boxes with the word!

go	get	got
got	go	get
go	got	go
get	go	got
go	get	go

Let's **go** swimming in the pool.
The water will be nice and cool!

go

Write a sentence using the word and draw a picture above!

. . . .

. . . .

. . . .

☆ Remember that a sentence begins with a capital letter and ends with a period! ☆

Trace the word and say it aloud:

has has has has has

Write the word:

_____

. . . .

_____

Complete the sentence with the word:

My monster____ one eye.

Grab a crayon and color the boxes with the word!

he	has	hat
have	he	has
hat	has	have
has	he	has
have	has	he

My monster **has** one eye.
Her favorite game is I spy.

has

Write a sentence using the word and draw a picture above!

. . . .

. . . .

. . . .

 Remember that a sentence begins with a capital letter and ends with a period!

have

Trace the word and say it aloud:

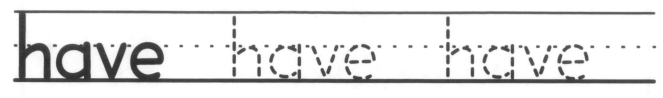

have   have   have

Write the word:

_____

. . . .

_____

Complete the sentence with the word:

We _____ watermelon.

Grab a crayon and color the boxes with the word!

has	he	have
he	have	has
have	hat	have
has	have	he
have	has	hat

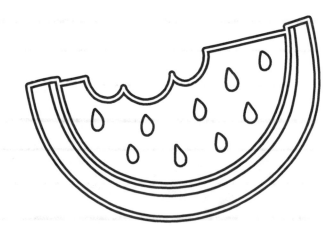

We **have** watermelon in a big slice. It is so sweet and nice!

have

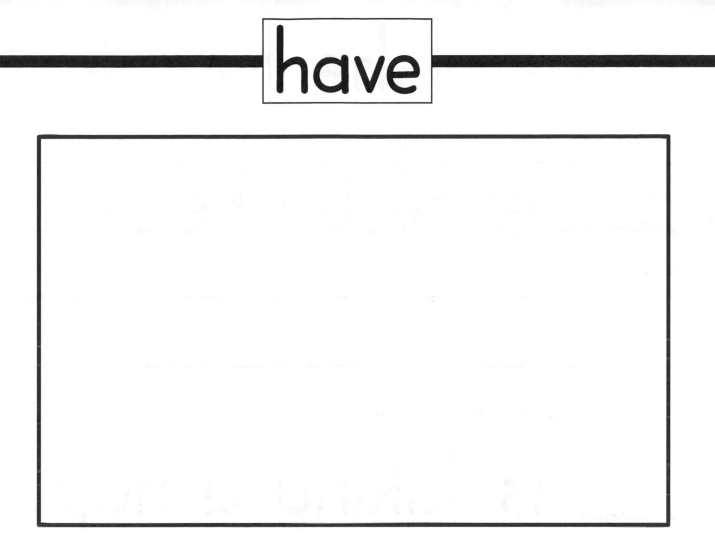

Write a sentence using the word and draw a picture above!

Trace the word and say it aloud:

he he he he he he

Write the word:

....

Complete the sentence with the word:

_____ is taking a nap.

Grab a crayon and color the boxes with the word!

have	has	he
he	hat	has
has	have	he
hat	he	has
have	has	he

He is taking a nap.
Of course, it is a catnap!

he

Write a sentence using the word and draw a picture above!

Remember that a sentence begins with a capital letter and ends with a period!

Trace the word and say it aloud:

here here here here

Write the word:

. . . .

Complete the sentence with the word:

_____ is my town.

Grab a crayon and color the boxes with the word!

have	has	here
here	hat	has
has	have	here
hat	here	has
have	has	here

Here is my town. Let me show you around!

here

Write a sentence using the word and draw a picture above!

Remember that a sentence begins with a capital letter and ends with a period!

I

Trace the word and say it aloud:

I I I I I I I I

Write the word:

Complete the sentence with the word:

__am five years old.

Grab a crayon and color the boxes with the word!

I	in	it
it	I	is
I	it	I
is	I	in
it	in	I

I am five years old today.
Hip Hip Hooray!

I

Write a sentence using the word and draw a picture above!

Remember that a sentence begins with a capital letter and ends with a period!

Trace the word and say it aloud:

in in in in in in in in

Write the word:

Complete the sentence with the word:

The sun is __ the sky.

Grab a crayon and color the boxes with the word!

I	in	it
it	I	in
in	it	I
is	I	in
it	in	I

The sun is **in** the sky. Up with the clouds, flying high.

in

Write a sentence using the word and draw a picture above!

_____

. . . .

_____

. . . .

_____

. . . .

_____

Remember that a sentence begins with a capital letter and ends with a period!

is

Trace the word and say it aloud:

is is is is is is is is is

Write the word:

. . . .

Complete the sentence with the word:

Paige ___ in school.

Grab a crayon and color the boxes with the word!

is	in	it
it	I	is
in	is	I
is	I	in
it	is	I

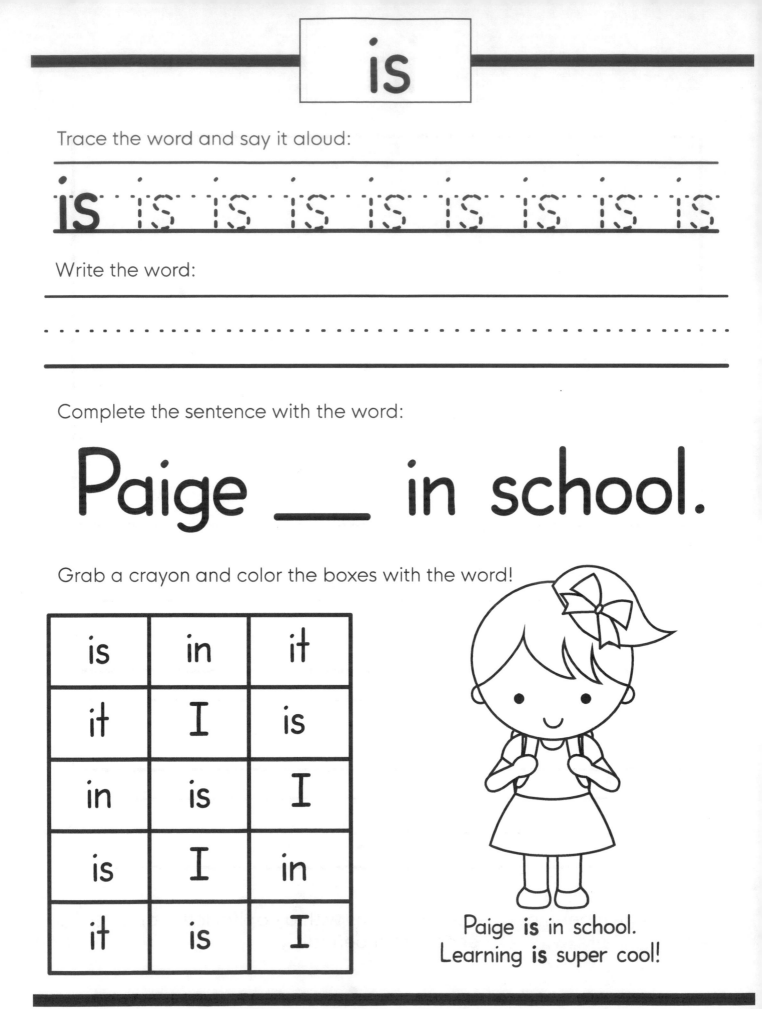

Paige **is** in school.
Learning **is** super cool!

is

Write a sentence using the word and draw a picture above!

Remember that a sentence begins with a capital letter and ends with a period!

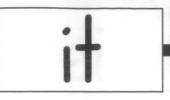

it

Trace the word and say it aloud:

it it it it it it it it it

Write the word:

Complete the sentence with the word:

___ is raining outside!

Grab a crayon and color the boxes with the word!

is	in	it
it	I	is
in	it	I
is	I	it
it	is	I

It is raining outside! Let's get under a blanket and hide!

it

Write a sentence using the word and draw a picture above!

. . . .

. . . .

. . . .

☆ Remember that a sentence begins with a capital letter and
ends with a period! ☆

Trace the word and say it aloud:

jump   jump   jump

Write the word:

Complete the sentence with the word:

Let's _____ like a deer!

Grab a crayon and color the boxes with the word!

jump	jam	jug
jug	jump	jam
jump	jam	jump
jug	jump	jam
jam	jug	jump

Let's **jump** like a deer! See how high you can clear!

jump

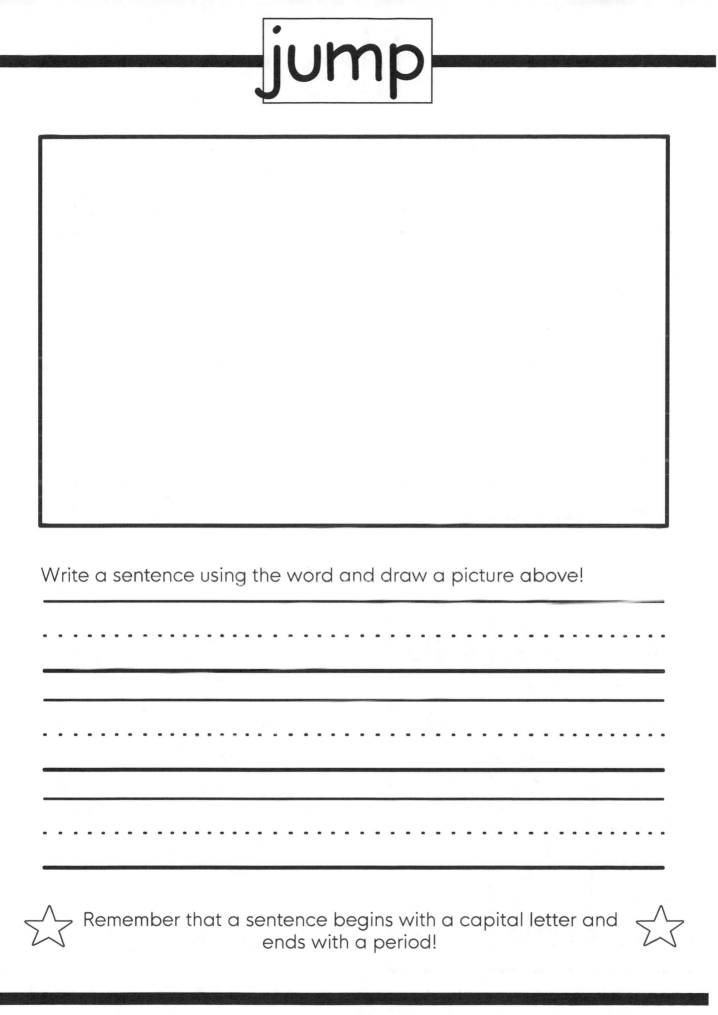

Write a sentence using the word and draw a picture above!

Remember that a sentence begins with a capital letter and ends with a period!

like

Trace the word and say it aloud:

like   like   like   like

Write the word:

Complete the sentence with the word:

I _____ shiny gems.

Grab a crayon and color the boxes with the word!

like	look	little
look	little	like
like	look	little
look	like	look
like	little	like

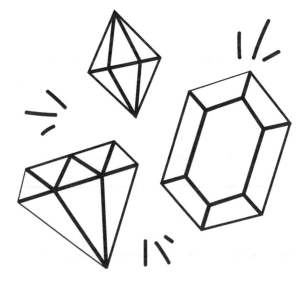

I **like** shiny gems, sparkling bright! What a sight!

like

Write a sentence using the word and draw a picture above!

. . . .

. . . .

. . . .

☆ Remember that a sentence begins with a capital letter and ends with a period! ☆

little

Trace the word and say it aloud:

little little little little

Write the word:

. . . .

Complete the sentence with the word:

Meet my _____ monster.

Grab a crayon and color the boxes with the word!

little	look	like
like	little	look
little	like	little
look	little	like
little	like	look

Meet my **little** monster, Sam.
His favorite food is ham!

little

Write a sentence using the word and draw a picture above!

Remember that a sentence begins with a capital letter and ends with a period!

look

Trace the word and say it aloud:

look look look look

Write the word:

_____

· ·

_____

Complete the sentence with the word:

_____ at my unicorn!

Grab a crayon and color the boxes with the word!

little	look	like
like	little	look
little	look	little
look	little	like
little	like	look

Look at my unicorn! She loves to play catch with her golden horn!

look

Write a sentence using the word and draw a picture above!

Remember that a sentence begins with a capital letter and ends with a period!

Trace the word and say it aloud:

me me me me me

Write the word:

Complete the sentence with the word:

Take ___ to the sea!

Grab a crayon and color the boxes with the word!

me	my	am
mat	me	my
me	my	am
me	mat	my
my	me	am

Take **me** to the sea! We can swim in the ocean and run free!

me

Write a sentence using the word and draw a picture above!

. . . .

. . . .

. . . .

☆ Remember that a sentence begins with a capital letter and ends with a period! ☆

my

Trace the word and say it aloud:

my my my my my

Write the word:

Complete the sentence with the word:

This is ___ pet dog.

Grab a crayon and color the boxes with the word!

my	me	am
am	my	mat
me	am	my
mat	my	me
my	me	am

This is **my** pet dog.
He jumps just like a frog!

my

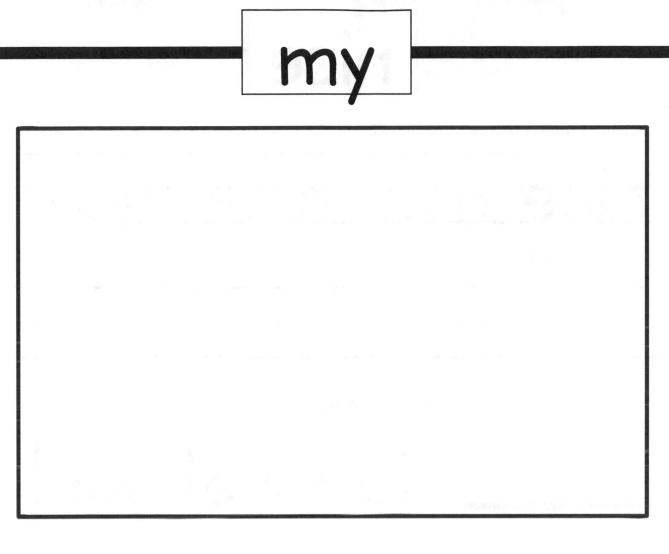

Write a sentence using the word and draw a picture above!

Remember that a sentence begins with a capital letter and ends with a period!

nice

Trace the word and say it aloud:

nice nice nice nice

Write the word:

. . . .

Complete the sentence with the word:

_____ to meet you!

Grab a crayon and color the boxes with the word!

nice	not	no
no	nice	not
in	no	nice
not	nice	in
nice	in	nice

Nice to meet you!
Will you be my friend, too?!

nice

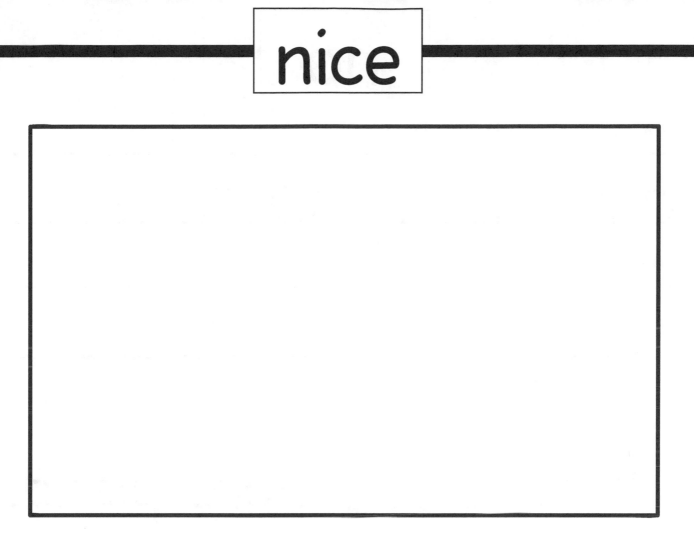

Write a sentence using the word and draw a picture above!

. . . .

. . . .

. . . .

☆ Remember that a sentence begins with a capital letter and
ends with a period! ☆

Trace the word and say it aloud:

no no no no no no

Write the word:

Complete the sentence with the word:

There is ___ more pizza.

Grab a crayon and color the boxes with the word!

not	no	nob
no	nob	not
nob	not	no
not	no	nob
no	not	no

There is **no** more pizza to eat.
I guess I'll just get a sweet!

no

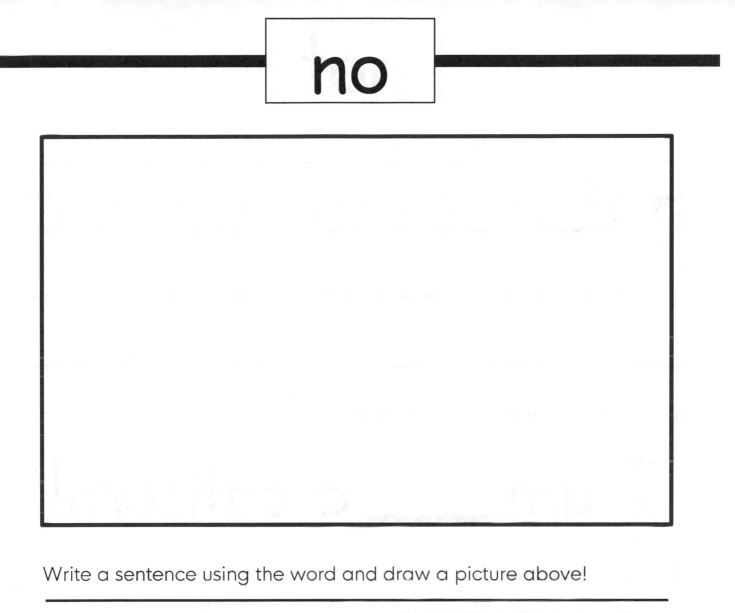

Write a sentence using the word and draw a picture above!

....

....

....

not

Trace the word and say it aloud:

not not not not not

Write the word:

Complete the sentence with the word:

I am ___ a caticorn!

Grab a crayon and color the boxes with the word!

not	no	nob
no	nob	not
nob	not	no
not	no	nob
no	not	no

I am not a caticorn! But if
I was, I'd have a rainbow horn!

not

Write a sentence using the word and draw a picture above!

Remember that a sentence begins with a capital letter and ends with a period!

one

Trace the word and say it aloud:

one one   one   one

Write the word:

· ·

Complete the sentence with the word:

I only see ____ fort.

Grab a crayon and color the boxes with the word!

one	on	no
no	one	on
one	on	one
no	one	on
one	no	one

I only see **one** fort. To enter, you must be on the royal court.

one

Write a sentence using the word and draw a picture above!

Remember that a sentence begins with a capital letter and
ends with a period!

our

Trace the word and say it aloud:

our   our   our   our

Write the word:

Complete the sentence with the word:

This is ____ house.

Grab a crayon and color the boxes with the word!

our	not	out
out	our	not
not	out	our
our	not	out
not	our	not

This is **our** house. It's much bigger than a mouse!

our

Write a sentence using the word and draw a picture above!

⭐ Remember that a sentence begins with a capital letter and ends with a period! ⭐

Trace the word and say it aloud:

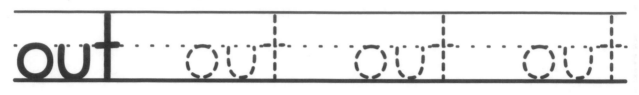

out   out   out   out

Write the word:

_____

· ·

_____

Complete the sentence with the word:

She is ____ in space.

Grab a crayon and color the boxes with the word!

our	not	out
out	our	not
not	out	our
our	not	out
not	our	not

She is **out** in space. One step forward for the human race!

out

Write a sentence using the word and draw a picture above!

⭐ Remember that a sentence begins with a capital letter and
ends with a period! ⭐

Trace the word and say it aloud:

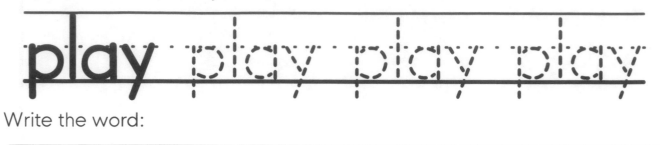

play play play play

Write the word:

Complete the sentence with the word:

I _____ in the ocean!

Grab a crayon and color the boxes with the word!

up	pan	play
play	pan	pal
up	pal	play
pal	play	up
play	pal	play

I **play** in the ocean! I like to **play** pretend in slow motion!

play

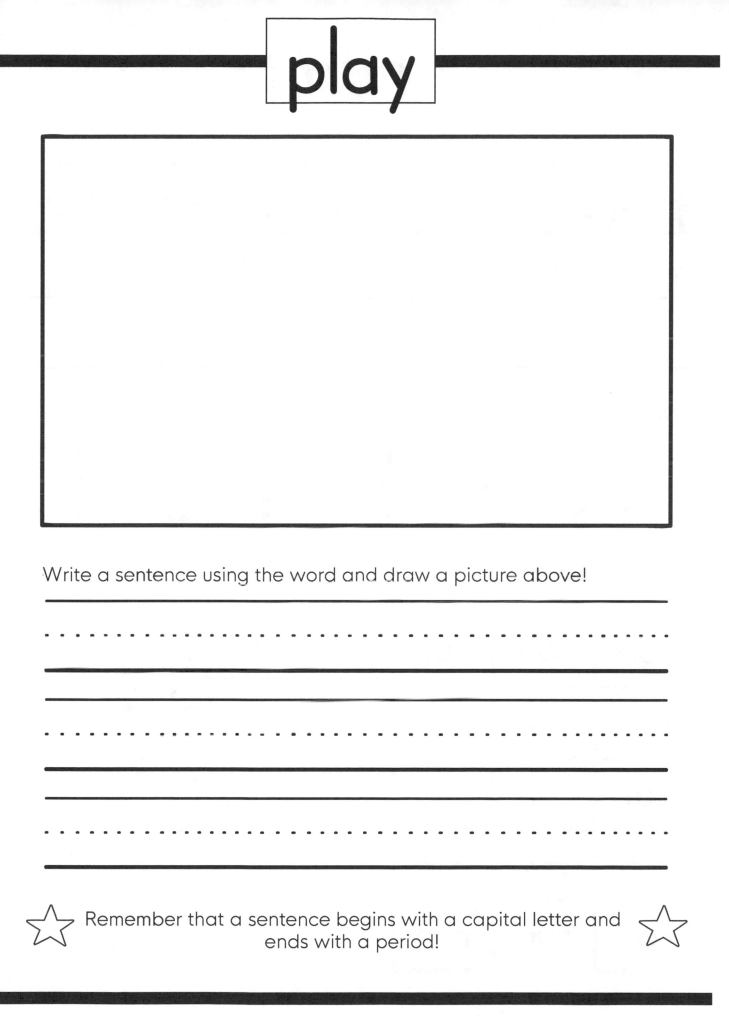

Write a sentence using the word and draw a picture above!

Remember that a sentence begins with a capital letter and ends with a period!

run

Trace the word and say it aloud:

run run run run run

Write the word:

Complete the sentence with the word:

Look at me ___ !

Grab a crayon and color the boxes with the word!

run	ran	rut
ran	run	rub
rut	run	ran
run	rut	run
ran	run	rub

Look at me **run**! I **run** in circles just for fun!

run

Write a sentence using the word and draw a picture above!

· ·

· ·

· ·

Remember that a sentence begins with a capital letter and ends with a period!

said

Trace the word and say it aloud:

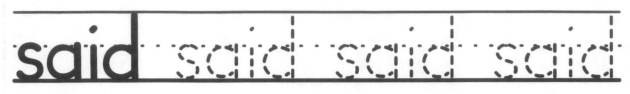

said said said said

Write the word:

_____

. . . .

_____

Complete the sentence with the word:

My unicorn _____ hi!

Grab a crayon and color the boxes with the word!

said	say	sad
sad	said	say
said	say	sad
say	sad	said
sad	said	say

My unicorn **said** hi! Then she taught me how to fly!

said

Write a sentence using the word and draw a picture above!

Remember that a sentence begins with a capital letter and ends with a period!

see

Trace the word and say it aloud:

see see see see see

Write the word:

Complete the sentence with the word:

I _____ a dinosaur!

Grab a crayon and color the boxes with the word!

see	set	sea
sea	see	set
set	sea	see
sea	see	set
see	set	see

I **see** a dinosaur! He likes
to shake it on the dance floor!

see

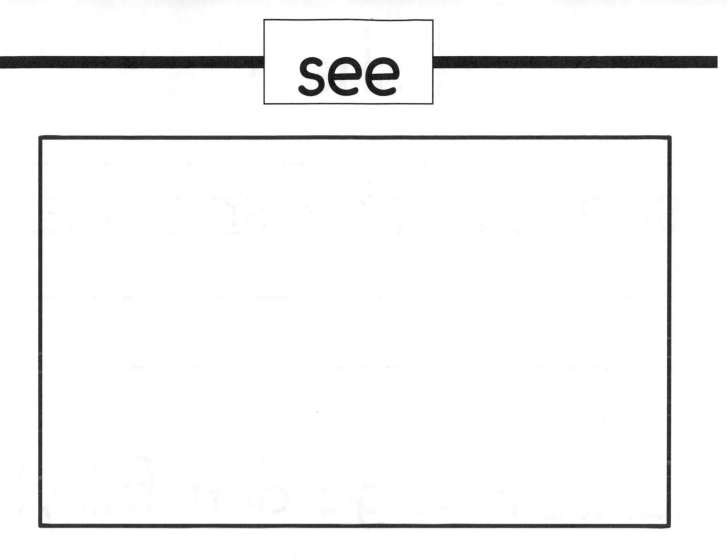

Write a sentence using the word and draw a picture above!

. . . .

. . . .

. . . .

☆ Remember that a sentence begins with a capital letter and ends with a period! ☆

she

Trace the word and say it aloud:

she she she she she

Write the word:

_____

. . . .

_____

Complete the sentence with the word:

_____ is a garden fairy!

Grab a crayon and color the boxes with the word!

she	see	shy
shy	she	see
see	shy	she
she	see	she
shy	she	see

She is a garden fairy! Her hair is the color of a strawberry!

she

Write a sentence using the word and draw a picture above!

_____

. . . .

_____

. . . .

_____

. . . .

_____

☆ Remember that a sentence begins with a capital letter and ends with a period! ☆

Trace the word and say it aloud:

the the the the the

Write the word:

Complete the sentence with the word:

Don't wake ___ owl!

Grab a crayon and color the boxes with the word!

the	then	them
them	the	then
the	then	the
them	the	then
the	then	the

Don't wake **the** owl! He will get mad and growl!

the

Write a sentence using the word and draw a picture above!

Remember that a sentence begins with a capital letter and ends with a period!

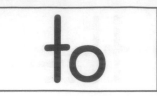

Trace the word and say it aloud:

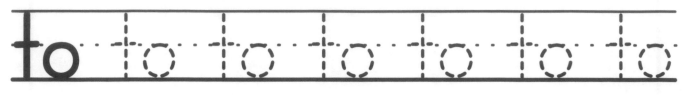

Write the word:

Complete the sentence with the word:

Let's go ___ the library.

Grab a crayon and color the boxes with the word!

tot	too	to
to	tot	too
too	to	tot
to	too	to
tot	to	too

Let's go **to** the library. I want a book about a giant blueberry!

to

Write a sentence using the word and draw a picture above!

· ·

_____

· ·

_____

· ·

_____

☆ Remember that a sentence begins with a capital letter and
ends with a period! ☆

up

Trace the word and say it aloud:

up ʊp ʊp ʊp ʊp ʊp

Write the word:

. . . .

Complete the sentence with the word:

Let's fly___to the sky!

Grab a crayon and color the boxes with the word!

up	us	pup
us	pup	up
us	up	us
up	pup	up
us	up	pup

Let's fly **up** to the sky! **Up** in the sky so high!

up

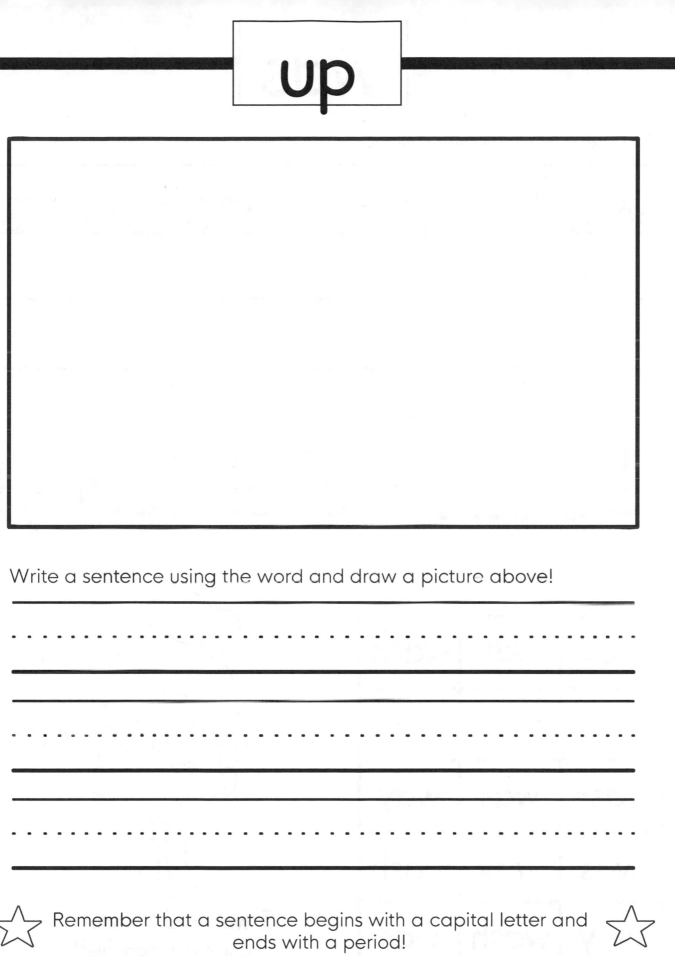

Write a sentence using the word and draw a picture above!

Trace the word and say it aloud:

was was was was

Write the word:

Complete the sentence with the word:

I _____ a chef today!

Grab a crayon and color the boxes with the word!

way	was	wash
was	way	was
wash	was	way
was	way	wash
way	wash	was

I **was** a chef today! I
cook a mean filet!

was

Write a sentence using the word and draw a picture above!

Trace the word and say it aloud:

we we we we we

Write the word:

....

Complete the sentence with the word:

_____ are friends!

Grab a crayon and color the boxes with the word!

we	went	wet
wet	we	went
went	wet	we
wet	we	went
we	wet	we

We are friends! **We** play together until the day ends!

we

Write a sentence using the word and draw a picture above!

_____

. . . .

_____

_____

. . . .

_____

_____

. . . .

_____

☆ Remember that a sentence begins with a capital letter and ends with a period! ☆

went

Trace the word and say it aloud:

went   went   went

Write the word:

Complete the sentence with the word:

We _____ to the zoo.

Grab a crayon and color the boxes with the word!

went	we	wet
wet	went	we
went	we	went
we	went	wet
wet	we	went

We **went** to the zoo. The baby giraffe is brand new!

went

Write a sentence using the word and draw a picture above!

Remember that a sentence begins with a capital letter and ends with a period!

Trace the word and say it aloud:

what · · · what · · · what

Write the word:

_____

· · · · · · · · · · · · · · · · · · ·

_____

Complete the sentence with the word:

_____ flavor did you get?

Grab a crayon and color the boxes with the word!

why	what	who
what	why	who
who	what	why
what	who	what
who	what	why

What flavor did you get? It is super yummy, I bet!

what

Write a sentence using the word and draw a picture above!

Remember that a sentence begins with a capital letter and ends with a period!

Trace the word and say it aloud:

where where where

Write the word:

Complete the sentence with the word:

_____ did you go?

Grab a crayon and color the boxes with the word!

where	when	where
were	where	when
when	were	where
where	when	were
were	where	when

Where did you go? To the other side of the rainbow?!

where

Write a sentence using the word and draw a picture above!

with

Trace the word and say it aloud:

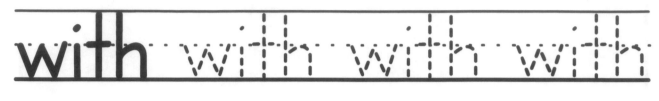

with with with with

Write the word:

_____

. . . .

_____

Complete the sentence with the word:

I'll play _____ you!

Grab a crayon and color the boxes with the word!

wit	with	witch
with	witch	wit
witch	wit	with
with	witch	wit
wit	with	witch

I'll play **with** you! Let's play
in the sand and the ocean, too!

with

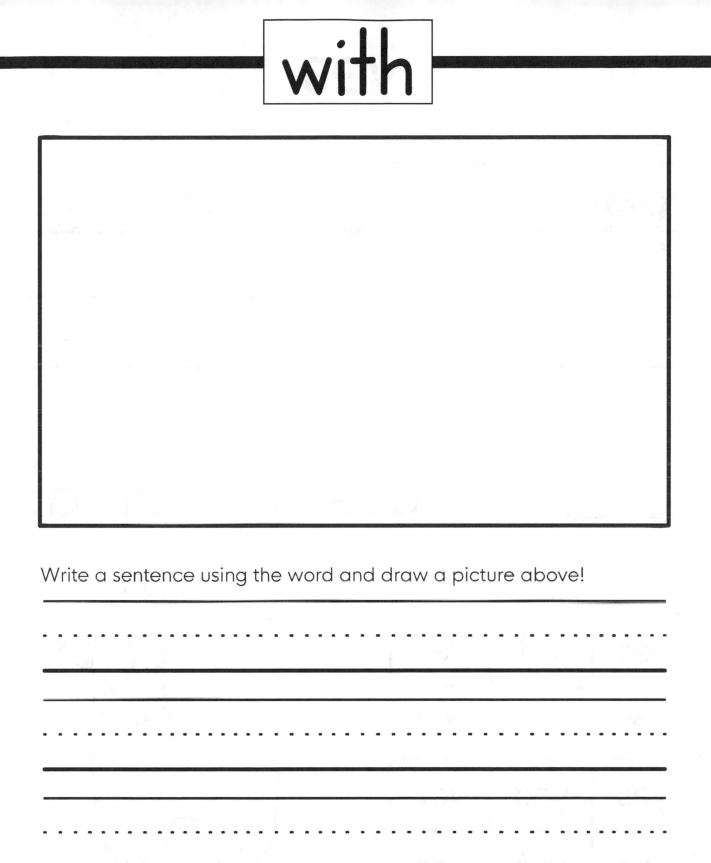

Write a sentence using the word and draw a picture above!

 Remember that a sentence begins with a capital letter and ends with a period!

yes

Trace the word and say it aloud:

yes yes yes yes yes

Write the word:

Complete the sentence with the word:

_____ , I love my llama!

Grab a crayon and color the boxes with the word!

yes	yet	yes
yet	yes	yea
yes	yea	yet
yea	yet	yes
yet	yes	yea

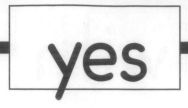

Yes, I love my llama! He
lives on our farm with his mama.

yes

Write a sentence using the word and draw a picture above!

....

_____

_____

....

_____

_____

....

_____

☆ Remember that a sentence begins with a capital letter and ends with a period! ☆

Trace the word and say it aloud:

you you you you

Write the word:

. . . .

Complete the sentence with the word:

_____ are magical, friend!

Grab a crayon and color the boxes with the word!

you	yum	yes
yes	you	yum
you	yum	you
yum	you	yes
you	yes	you

You are magical, friend! Can **you** come over this weekend?

you

Write a sentence using the word and draw a picture above!

Remember that a sentence begins with a capital letter and ends with a period!

Made in United States
Troutdale, OR
01/08/2024

16813495R00060